LET'S LOOK
Flowers

Nicola Tuxworth

LORENZ BOOKS

Flowers everywhere

Flowers grow in all sorts of different places.

petal

Indoor flowers
Some flowers will grow indoors.

leaf

stem

geranium

thistle

Wild flowers
Wild flowers grow in the countryside or on waste ground.

dandelion

rose

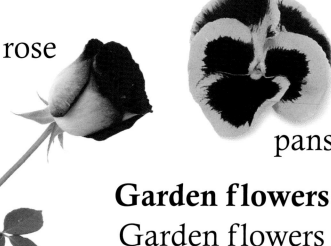

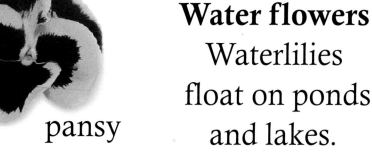

pansy

Water flowers
Waterlilies
float on ponds
and lakes.

Garden flowers
Garden flowers
are grown in parks
and gardens.

cherry
blossom

**Flowers
on trees**
Some trees
flower in
the spring.

How do flowers grow?

Flowers need sunlight and air. They also need water, which they drink through their roots.

flower

leaf

soil

roots

chrysanthemum

Sunlight
Sunlight helps plants to grow strong.

Rain
When it rains the soil gets wet. Flowers drink the water from the soil.

Colorful flowers

Flowers can be almost any color. Which colors can you see?

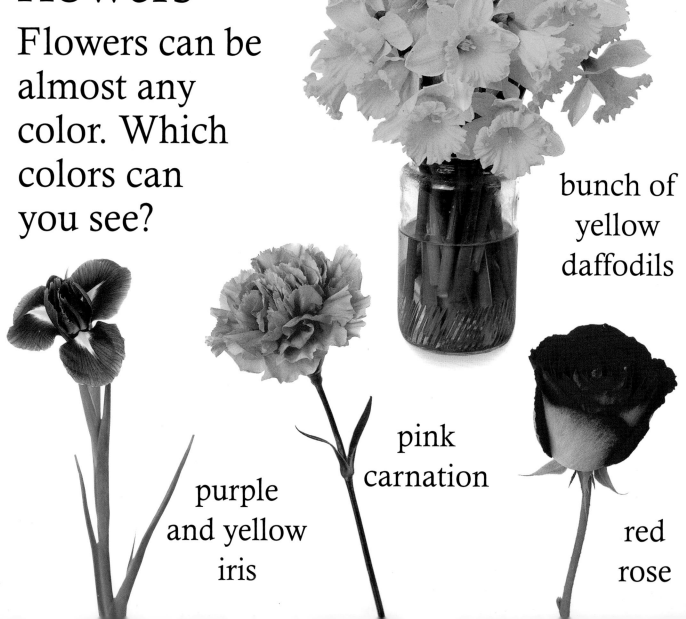

bunch of yellow daffodils

purple and yellow iris

pink carnation

red rose

deep purple
anemone

pink and
white lily

bright orange
chrysanthemums

Flowers all year round

Different flowers grow at different times of the year.

Spring flowers

daffodil

freesia

Summer flowers

sunflower

chrysanthemums

Autumn flowers

dahlia

scabious

Winter flower

winter pansy

flower
bud

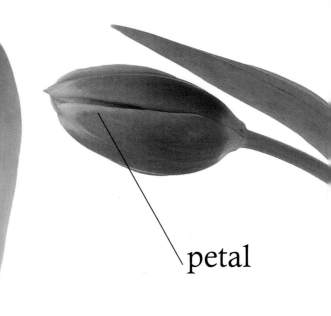

petal

Bursting
into flower

Most flowers
take a while
to open.

The tulip
flower is curled
up inside this
small bud.

Can you see the petals beginning to open? What color are they?

Now the tulip flower is fully open. What colors can you see?

petal

stem

Seeds and bulbs

Some flowers grow from seeds. Others grow from bulbs.

golden tulip bulbs

wrinkled gladioli bulbs

smooth fava bean seeds

striped sunflower seeds

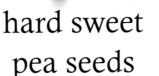

hard sweet pea seeds

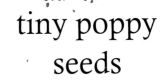

tiny poppy seeds

black scallion
seeds

brown
tomato seeds

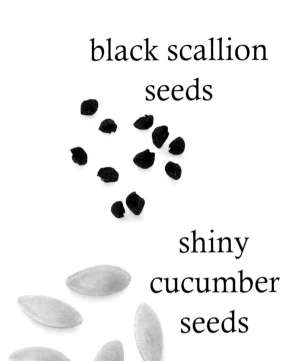

round
radish seeds

pale lettuce
seeds

shiny
cucumber
seeds

mottled green
bean seeds

Have you seen any of
these seeds or bulbs?

Flowers and food

Some flowers turn into fruit and vegetables for us to eat.

strawberry flowers

strawberries

apple blossom

pears

pear blossom

apples

runner bean
flowers

runner
beans

blackberry flowers
and blackberries

zucchini
plant

zucchini

Animal visitors

Birds, bees and butterflies
all like to visit flowers.

Honey bees
collect
yellow
pollen from
flowers.

Some flowers turn into berries. The berries make a tasty feast for birds.

Butterflies like to sip the sweet juice inside flowers.

Growing flowers

You can grow flowers easily in a window box or a pot.

watering can

daffodils

patio roses

crocuses

polyanthus

A cactus is easy to care for.

Try planting the seeds from fruit.

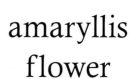

amaryllis flower

This amazing flower will grow on your windowsill.

Flowers for sale

Look at
these roses.
How many
different
colors can
you see?